The Million Dollar Equation:

How to build a million dollar business in 3
years or less

RICHELLE SHAW

RTS PUBLISHING, LLC

Henderson, Nevada

RTS Publishing, LLC

1489 W. Warm Springs Rd., Ste 110

Henderson, NV 89014

For information regarding special discounts for bulk purchases,

Please contact RTS Publishing, LLC

702-966-8410 or nevadamarketingcenter@gmail.com

Manufactured in the United States of America

10 9 8

Library of Congress Cataloging-in-Publication Data is available

ISBN **978-1475191486**

Visit Ms. Shaw at   http://www.RichelleShaw.com

ACKNOWLEDGEMENTS

First and foremost, I would like to say THANK YOU to my Lord and Savior Jesus Christ. Through it all, I have to love this journey because it helped me become closer to God. I have been so blessed, even after 9-11 tragedies, I found myself saying thank You Lord, after the 2 deaths, I said, thank You Lord and then when the guy didn't pay me – whew, thank You Lord. Because of You Lord, through all of the valleys, I never wanted for ANYTHING. I remember one day very clearly. I was afraid to answer the phone or my front door.

I was sitting in front of my computer and my doorbell rang. I decided to not answer it because it could only be bad news. I heard my dog barking and barking, so I looked out the window and saw the Gas Company Truck parked out front. I thought, oh no, they might have turned off my gas. I ran outside and stopped the service guy in my driveway and, yes he had turned it off. I asked him, could he turn it back on and he said, hey, I rang the doorbell. The bill was less than $40, and I wanted to give you the opportunity to pay. Sigh. The $40 past due balance turned into $190 because of a $150 deposit now required to reconnect the service.

Boy, I needed a FreshStart Gas Company ☺ that did not require a deposit.

For 18 days, I went without gas. That meant, no cooking on the stove. No hot water. We pulled out a housewarming gift which was an electric skillet and began preparing meals on it. But when I knew for sure God was carrying me, I ran the water for my bath and it was warm – without heat??? Only God could make the cold water warm. Thank You, God for consistently providing for me.

My God had an opportunity to show up and show out in my life so many times, throughout this journey, I just want to encourage you, if you do not know Him, you should get to know Him. Because, without God, you will want to give up on this entrepreneurial journey. But with God, I always knew that I had a bigger purpose and when I share my gifts with the world, my life would be a blessing to others.

Thank you to my family who has also been my rock and is the reason I make all decisions, all decisions to run, to fight, to retreat, to love. I thank them for always supporting me.

Thank you to my Mother, Janie Mae for being my foundation – who truly drives me crazy, but only because she loves me and wants the best for me. She is PURE comedy too. AND I love her to pieces for looking at me every morning and telling me that I am beautiful! As Devyn and I leave each morning she says – you both look cute! Gotta love that!

Thank you to my father, sister, brother, cousins, aunts, uncles all 117 of y'all, I love you!

Dear Devyn – You are the BEST thing to EVER happen to ME in my WHOLE LIFE! No YOU Devyn!!! I love saying this everyday and every night to my little SUNSHINE. WOW, I love that little girl. She is the air I breathe and it makes me understand my Mom so much more now.

Thank you to my special friends, who accept my calls in the middle of the night, who have just met me and the ones who have chased me for 30 years. I thank you for all of your support.

Thank YOU!

Also by *R I C H E L L E   S H A W*

How to Build A Million Dollar Business in Las Vegas – Without the Casinos

Overcome – Obstacles, What Obstacles? (March, 2013)

Table of Contents

Introduction

Hi, First of all let me say thank you for entrusting your business journey to me. I realize this is simply my audition, however, I am positive this information is worth the investment. We should start with some premises:

1. Even though this is exactly what I used to build my million dollar business, the lawyers have asked for a disclaimer – here it is. Implementing every idea from this book may not result in a million dollar business however, it's the only way I know to build one.

2. By just reading this book – nothing will happen. Obvious right, however, it's important to say

3. Lastly, the way you look at your business will change dramatically after you complete the exercises in this book.

Now let's begin

We should start with my story. My name is Richelle Shaw and for many years, I was the only female African American Public Utility owner in the United States. I owned a telephone company. How did that happen? I was dating 3 men in 3 different states and I had an enormous telephone bill. I was working for a 100% commission only advertising sales job and I have to admit I was a horrible sales person. I was afraid to get out of the car. At one point I even hired my best friend to ride in the car with me so that I could close the sale. I was afraid to return to people who asked me to return for the full presentation. I tell you about being afraid because that was when, I decided that I needed to get business to come to me. Now that I advise and coach entrepreneurs – they all tell me that if the customer would just come to them, it would be so much easier.

Well if this is true for you, I have the systems that I used to not only get them to come to me but when they arrive they were primed and ready to buy.

But back to my story. I told you that I was unable to sell very well, but one thing about selling telephone service, I never had to ask for a check. I just had to ask if the prospect was ready to switch service. I was promoted to Director of Sales, then, to Director of Operations, Vice President of Operations and Executive Vice President from $300,000 to $36 million and then I bought the business from my boss. 52 employees and $1 million per month customers were my day to day life. And then, September 11, 2001 changed my entire business. In the telephone business, the clock is always ticking, ticking from the time the call is made, it takes 30 days to receive and process all of the call records, then 30 days to get the invoice to the customer and the customer of course gets 30 days to pay before it is late.

On Sept. 11, the world changed and so did my business. Customers lost their businesses, on-time payers became slow payers and slow payers became outrageous. There is a fine line between, when to disconnect service. As my aunt used to tell the credit card companies, "ummmm, if I didn't pay you when I was able to use the credit card, what makes you think that now that you have restricted access, that I am going to pay it. " That is exactly why it was difficult to disconnect customers. Disconnecting was an admission of defeat and acceptance that there was a 75% chance that I was never going to get paid. My staff did everything to work with the customer, however, within 90 days, the business, my company unraveled.

My first book – How to Build a Million Dollar Business in Las Vegas – Without the Casinos, I chronicle the journey of recovery of what happened after I lost it all and how I rebuilt my million dollar business in less than 6 months. I used the Million Dollar Equation systems to rebuild FreshStart Telephone.

I wish I could tell you that I rebuilt my company because I was sure that I knew how to build million dollar businesses. I read an article about getting a job and what to expect via the timeline. It stated that it takes 1 month for every $10,000 earned. Right before I bought the company, I was earning, $22,000 per month. Yikes, it was going to take 22 months to find a job. Well, while I was submitting resumes I decided to try one more time to build this business.

By implementing each of these systems, it worked? It worked. It worked! Again, in all fairness, I wish I could tell you that I was so confident this was going to work. I tried to implement everything that I read and saw. I tried everything because I had nothing to lose. I had already filed bankruptcy, what else could happen to me.

Life after writing about building a million dollar business – was unnerving. Business was fun, the fun side made me happy. Big things were happening.

What happened to FreshStart Telephone?

At first, it was coasting along. I reached a crossroads. I needed to make a decision about growing the business. In order to grow to the $10 million mark, I was going to have to decide between, adding new infrastructure, investing into new technology or partnering with a bigger company. Partners are for dancing and I had not much success working with others larger companies.

I firmly believe that if your business is not growing its dying. My growth was stagnant and if it was to grow, I needed lots of capital. I thought about loans but thus far, had built the company debt free. I had to make a decision.

Unfortunately, The DECISION became easier

I got a call from my fiancé that his sister was in a car accident. His sister was 9 months pregnant and after having 3 boys, she was finally pregnant with a girl. She was driving to pick up her husband after work, during a rain storm and a truck ran her off the road. We rushed to the funeral in Houston, Texas and vowed as a family that we would stay together and not go so long without seeing each other. We bonded together and held each other and seemed ok, after the long week away.

I was scheduled to attend a conference in Chicago so I flew from Houston to Chicago and my fiancé flew from Chicago to Las Vegas. 1am in the morning, I received a call. It was my fiancé screaming that it happened again. His other sister was driving home from Houston to return to Oklahoma. On the highway, a truck driver changed lanes and did not see her SUV. The SUV and the truck collided. During the accident, the truck flipped and fatally injured his other sister and her daughter. Three other passengers survived but were injured too. So within 9 days, we lost 4 close family members.

At that point, I decided I have this precious little girl – I was looking at what was important in my life and I decided that the most important thing was not working 24/7, but to spend the time with my daughter.

My competitor had been chasing me for years to purchase my company. He had purchased another company from me and paid me monthly for 8 years. So the thought of being paid, monthly to enjoy my daughter sounded like the best of both worlds. I made the decision to sell. I was vulnerable, I just wanted it over. It was actually the best deal for me at the time. I was still grieving and stressing about balancing my life with my business life and I had given up trying to work it out.

During a HUGE combination of errors, I received one payment for my million dollar company. There was no suing, because the buyer lost both my company and his company within 90 days.

I said, God really? Again? I went through my savings everything. I was too exhausted to rebuild again. Or was I? I started telling myself that, FreshStart was a fluke. I convinced myself that as much as I think I know what I am doing, maybe I don't.

Now imagine, I had been speaking on book tours, teaching entrepreneurs who asked for more help while still owning the telephone company. Now, it deflated my confidence. I realize now that I gave up. I actually QUIT. And out of the blue, I received a coaching application from an ob/gyn doctor who needed help with his practice. His application was really 5 pages of begging me to help him with his business.

I thought, really, no one wakes up in the morning excited to go to the gynecologist. What in the world am I going to do to build his business? Because I needed the money, I agreed to a consultation. He actually canceled the consultation because he said their computer system was down and he wanted me to see it in action. The cancelation of course convinced me that he was stalling and did not want to pay me. My confidence was rocked.

But, he called the next week and I went out for the consultation. I wasn't even sure what to take to the consultation. So I took a file folder with his completed "begging" forms. I sat in his lobby scared to death, thinking somebody is going to find out that I have no idea what I am doing. Then, I watched as a patient arrived to see the doctor and one by one, the suggestions to improve his business, the employee flow, and his marketing exploded out of me. The file folder had over 100 items that I felt needed to be implemented. Now the problem, how do I give him my suggestions?

I went back to my house and started typing up the suggestions. They were broken down into different categories and by priority of how I would implement them, if it was my company. To my surprise the doctor said, well can you just do it?

I had the time, and remember needed the money so when he agreed to the amount I asked for, I fell to the ground and cried my eyes out. BUT, if I have to confess… I was scared again as to how was I going to deliver.

We started April 1st implementation of the plan and I just kept implementing like I did at FreshStart. By the end of the year, we were cruising along with new patients, the doctor was crazy busy, lots of referrals – even one month we received 157 new patients. It was now January and I thought, ohhh, it would be nice to know what were the numbers. So I asked, hey – how did we do, what was the end of the year revenue? I remember the text like yesterday. We started at $384,000 and our end of the year the revenue number was $1.1. WOW, 9 months from $384k to $1.1million.

My confidence was back. If these systems can sell a pap smear, what couldn't it sell. Fast Forward... I received lots of doctors referrals, even a gynecologic oncologist. What?? It even works for a cancer doctor. Then, I implemented the million dollar equation with a periodontist, optometrist, auto repair, online membership site for lovers, seminar company, school, with 93 different industries.

No more thinking it was a fluke, no more lack of confidence. This stuff works. Implemented, it is the best cure for an ailing business and the ultimate way to change your life by creating a sustainable, predictable business with systems to create a sought after asset. What an amazing journey to actually believing that I have a system. I realize now after going through it, I believe that the reason why the buyer of FreshStart defaulted, was because, God knew that I would have stopped everything. I would not have started consulting. I would have allowed my work life to stop. It was because I quit, instead of transitioned. God knew I was not ready to quit so He orchestrated a way so that I would discover my true gift. Now I am clear that sharing my experiences with you is what I am supposed to be doing.

Your $550 worth of FREE Training is available to you now. Simply go to http://www.MDENation.com – The Premier Community for Building Your Business Quickly. Now, Let's Get to WORK!

Your Business Needs The Million Dollar Equation

My goal is to transform your business from the small little side hobby generating under $100,000 to a really full-fledged million dollar enterprise. The best thing about it is, that's what I'm an expert at! The Million Dollar Equation will help give you the freedom to do what you want to do with your children, with your family, and more. This all starts with you creating a business that is much bigger than you. Currently you are thinking about the product and the service instead of what the big picture is and what this means for you, your business and your lifestyle.

Typically, when I coach business owners, they are thinking too small! They are thinking about just being able to pay their bills or being able to generate an extra few dollars, instead of being focused on generating a solution to a specific problem. Helping people worldwide and being a conduit to happiness should be YOUR ultimate goal. Currently, every day I read to myself my goals, "My vision for my business is that I'm serving millions of people, helping 1 million business owners create their own million dollar dream businesses and lifestyles. My mission is helping business owners develop simple but specific business plans to build million dollar businesses. I am more focused on answering the question, what is my goal in life, than how to pay bills.

You might be thinking to yourself that all you do is sell a product or service – but that is not what you do. It's about the bigger picture. In this Million Dollar Equation I am going to require that you take some risks. I'm going to encourage you to do things that you don't like to do. You may know a lot of this stuff, but you've just chosen not to do it because you don't feel comfortable doing it. Building a million dollar business means that you need to feel uncomfortable. You need to get into the habit of doing things that make you kind of nervous and a little scared. You are going to have to take some chances. But the rewards are worth it!

Let's start out with what you should expect. What you should expect is to win. You should expect that when all of this is over, you've got a template that you can use into your existing and your next business. I do all the things that I tell you about, I do them instinctively. So instead of making up excuses just implement what you read in this book. Alright, let me tell you one last thing, you are going to have to work. I'm going to need you to take these examples and put them into your own business.

I want you to spend some time working on your business because once we complete the MDE Action Plan, then it's just about you pulling the trigger and implementing each task. What keeps you from pulling the trigger? You don't know what to do and the things you know to do, you are scared to do. You are scared to invest. You are scared to take risks. You are scared to take a chance. But through the Million Dollar Equation, I'm going to give you the confidence to take action. With that confidence comes success. The success of generating consistent income will make you can say, it was worth the work! Finally, if you are scared to take risks, Go BACK to WORK! A funny story, in college, I wanted to be a standup comedian. I was funny and people would say "I missed my calling". I had a chance to ask Eddie Murphy about standup and he asked me what was my backup plan. I told him, I was attending UCLA and he told me to stay there and get a job. I was crushed. I asked was it my comedy? He said, no, but this business is so tough, that if you have a backup plan, you will use it. I feel the same way now about building a business.

This book is broken down into specific chapters based on my proven formula to building a million dollar business called The Million Dollar Equation. Briefly let me explain each piece of the equation.

$$(1GS+TM+MC+FU) + (RET+REA+REF) \times 85W + 3GR$$

1GS = One GREAT SOLUTION – Your business needs to solve a problem.

TM = TARGET MARKET – These are the customers that have the problem you are solving with your GREAT SOLUTION.

MC = MARKETING CALENDAR – Consistent implementation generates consistent income.

FU = FOLLOW UP – Each prospect or customer should have a calculated FOLLOW UP system to help convert every prospect into a customer and every customer to spend more money and become more valuable.

RET = Retention – Imagine if every customer you ever sold was still doing business with you. This section focuses on keeping, growing and expanding your customers for life.

REA = Reactivation – The 2nd easiest customer to sell is an old customer. This portion of the equation helps you generate an immediate cash flow surge.

REF = Referral – The 3rd easies customer to sell is a referral customer. This section details when, who and how to ask for referrals.

85W = 85 Ways to Get a New Customer – I was inspired by a story I read based on the theory, "Diversity Leads to Stability" and at the end I determined that I did not know 1 way to get 85 customers but I know 85 ways to get one!

3GR = There are ONLY 3 Ways to Grow a Business – In this section I explain how to leverage these 3 ways and which ones to focus on in priority.

BONUS = The Accelerators - OPC – Other People's Customers and the power of Joint Ventures,   AP – Affluent Prices – how to charge more and why you don't want to be Walmart – The "Low Price Leader", CI – Continuity Income – The only way to get RICH, get paid automatically.

MDE is a series of systems to move your business forward automatically. How to read this book – depending on where your business is currently, you may want to jump ahead to REA to get a cash flow surge or 85W to get additional ways to get a new customer. But I would suggest that after teaching and coaching entrepreneurs for 7 years, starting at the beginning is truly the best way. The 1GS & TM are the hardest chapters to grasp, however once you have CLARITY on those 2 pieces, the implementation is easier and the results from your efforts are more lucrative.

Chapter 1: One GREAT SOLUTION
Solving the Big Problem
The Biggest, Essential Piece of the Million Dollar Equation

GS = Your GREAT SOLUTION

The GREAT SOLUTION & TARGET MARKET (in Chapter 2) are the first place to start, once you get this piece down in The Million Dollar Equation, it is going to make everything else flow easily in your business. I have been coaching and consulting of 7 years and the first thing that I look at in a business is their GREAT SOLUTION. When I ask business owners, "What is your GREAT SOLUTION?"

they often say "oh…" and they tell me something foolish from 7th grade English class.

Your business must be able to solve a big problem with your TARGET MARKET in order to get people to respond and buy quickly. If you do not do this part correctly, you may get people to respond, you can even make some money, but they won't respond quickly to your product or service offers or become raving fans of your business. We want them responding quickly and pay top dollar and to be out telling other people about your business. If you have a product that people are not out telling everybody else about, it is because you have not given them the proper tools nor have you shown what problem your business is actually solving.

MDE RULE #1 Your business must solve a problem for your prospect

If your business isn't fixing the potential customer's problem, the business will never reach the million dollar level, without a significant investment and advertising budget. Without a GREAT SOLUTION, we would need a minimum $1 million investment. Remember the Dot.com boom? There were some companies that invested millions and millions of dollars without breaking the million dollar sales level. But if you start solving a problem, then it is going to change everything. Start UP Entrepreneurs try to make this so complicated. They tell me, "Oh, I need to have a website" "I need to have video on the website" "I need to have audio" "Oh I need to have a business card" or "Oh I need a brochure." Those are distracting you from understanding that when you solve a problem, you can build a business very quickly with little money, and little tools. So, before investing in expensive websites or 4-color brochure printing, describe the GREAT SOLUTION and communicate it throughout the tools and the customers will come to you.

Communicating The GREAT SOLUTION

My company – FreshStart Telephone started as a solution without a website, without business cards just communicating the new offering to prospects. Present your GREAT SOLUTION whenever you communicate with potential prospects and customers. When you give your prospect the GREAT SOLUTION for your business, you want them to say, "Really? How do you do that?" And when they do – you should smile from ear to ear, because that is the signal that the Great Solution for your business worked.

In your business, as you start to think about what problems you solve, begin by reviewing what problems your customers are experiencing. If you are a brand new startup, gather a focus group that contains similar members of your desired target market. For businesses with existing clients, it is easier to determine what customers want and what you should be selling to them and how to communicate it. When you start having conversations they will tell you the problems they need solved. So what was their big problem? Use surveys in your business to determine what problem you are solving.

MDE RULE #2 Survey Your Prospects - Easiest way to discover what problem you should be solving, ASK Them!

When you talk to clients, if you find out you are not solving their problem or at the very least unable to give them the confidence that you can solve their problem, then they are never going to buy. They are going to say "Oh, let me think about it" and then you'll find out that they bought it from somebody else. It has absolutely nothing to do with your product or service. It has to do with the problem that you are solving. Once you get that determined, it will change everything.

For start-ups – start by looking at your industry and list the problems that need to be solved. You can also survey potential prospects that fit into your TARGET MARKET to see what's missing. Then, simply, create your product or service to solve the problem.

The FreshStart Solution – My Telephone Company's GREAT SOLUTION

Let's talk about how I came up with FreshStart Telephone and apply it in your own business. Here's what happened. I met this guy, you know, all of my stories revolve around 'I met this guy.' So met this guy who owned a bankruptcy company and it's called FreshStart. I was about to file bankruptcy and I wanted his expertise.

I said, "Do you think I could sell my telephone service to the people that you have?" He said, "Yeah, you know what? That might be a good collaboration."

At this time, I didn't have a sales force and I was targeting different residential customers. Now, was I going to go knock on doors? No, I wasn't knocking on anybody's door. I had to figure out a way to communicate my message to the TARGET MARKET. I discovered the biggest fear for my potential previously bankrupt credit challenged prospects was to have their telephone disconnected. So, my solution became – With FreshStart Telephone, you never have to worry about disconnected again. In talking to prospects, their eyes lit up when I told them they would never have to worry about being disconnected again. When I started to tell that to prospects, the response was, "Really, how do you do that?" *Ahhhh, the magic question you want!*

I would respond, "Here's what we do… We make sure you have no surprise billing and your bill is the same amount every month. Here's the problem you are having with your current phone service when you receive the bill you are scared to open it. We make sure that you never get disconnected again".

My clients' big problem is that they were getting disconnected and they were unable to reach their family. Now my GREAT SOLUTION to never get disconnected again with flat rate billing. I gave them flat rate billing, no surprise billing, a consistent due date so they had no more excuses. The due date never changed. Their bills were due on the 1st, late on the 3rd, and on the 6th if they hadn't paid me, they were disconnected. When the customer came to sign up, we would tell them, "Oh it's great, well guess what, your bill is due on the 1st" and they would instantly say back to us, "Oh, that's perfect. My rent's due on the first." We replied, "Great, it's late on the 3rd." "Yeah, well that's when my rent's late." And we say, "And we disconnect you on the 6th." They go, "Ooh yeah, just like my rent. I get evicted if I don't pay my rent then too."

The customer began to make deals with themselves in their heads and it wasn't about me selling them at

> *How can you apply these strategies in your business?*
>
> 1. *Use an experience*
> 2. *Create the solution*
> 3. *Test the solution*

that point. When you get the GREAT SOLUTION right, when you solve a big problem, you don't have to overcome objections. What happens is the prospect is so excited about you solving their problem that they start to tell you how your product works for them. Your customer discovers that your product is the best thing for them, which removes all barriers to selling. We also offered a no credit check, no deposit to sweeten the deal, which made sales soar and I rebuilt my million dollar business back within 5 months!

McDonald's GREAT SOLUTION

It's not about how great the food is. If it's about how good the food is, then why is McDonalds still in business? My kid loves to go to McDonald's because she gets to play on the little playground that's there. She gets to eat French fries.

She gets to feed herself, which when she was little, that was a big deal.

But that is why they are open. It's not about the food. It's about the toy. It's about the experience. It's about the kid every time they see the arches crying, "Mom, I can't wait to go to McDonald's" and you want your clients, your patients, your customers, to feel this same way.

Finding Your GREAT SOLUTION

Look at your industry and do what is different, because that's going to set you apart. There is always going to be competition. So if everybody in your industry is selling in bundles, then I want you to break up the bundles. Make two separate products so that now when they try to compare you, they are not comparing apples to apples. They are comparing apples to oranges. So that's going to be the first thing that helps you provide the GREAT SOLUTION. If your competitors are selling it individually, then I want you to create a bundle.

The next thing, create a survey to your existing customers or create a question on Facebook. Facebook has a place where you can ask a question now and get the answers so that you can formulate your GREAT SOLUTION. Once you get what the problems are, start asking prospects how they feel about the problems. You must be able to solve a big problem in your business in order to get people to respond quickly.

MDE RULE #1 – *You must solve a problem for your prospect.*

MDE RULE #2 – *Survey your prospects to determine what problem to solve*

MDE RULE #3 – *Determine the problem, create the GREAT SOLUTION, and sell millions!*

Chapter 2: TARGET MARKET – Who in the World is Your Solution For?

Once you know your GREAT SOLUTION discovering your TARGET MARKET is easy. But first if you have not completely figured out your GREAT SOLUTION, sometimes you can start with your TARGET MARKET and then create your GREAT SOLUTION. So, let's start with picking a TARGET MARKET in case you are having trouble with your GREAT SOLUTION and then solve the TARGET MARKET's problem.

What makes a great TARGET MARKET is that it's specific, not generic. So if you say all women, you don't have enough money to reach them. All women cannot be your TARGET MARKET. It's got to be something specific.

A Specific TARGET MARKET

Ideal TARGET MARKET
1. Be specific, not generic
2. A group that is reachable
3. Big enough to have their own media
4. Small enough that big competition doesn't want them
5. Have a big problem that needs to be solved
6. A market that will buy

For example the OB/GYN doctor I helped build his physician practice from $300,000 to $1.2 million in nine months. First we picked a TARGET MARKET of women in Las Vegas between the ages of 35 and 45. . Then we researched problems specifically related to these women which lead to weight gain, fatigue, mood swings, loss of libido, hormonal imbalances and hormonal challenges. That's where we spend the majority of our marketing dollars. Once we focused on women between 35 and 45, we started looking at what keeps them up at night or what makes them feel horrible. What kept them up at night are their imbalanced hormones. Their adrenals glands are not balanced which caused insomnia. The majority of these women were likely either premenopausal or they are going through menopause. Our solution – Bio-Identical hormones replacement therapy endorsed by Opera and Suzanne Somers, that within 2 weeks, helped women between 35 to 45 feel better, look good and have great sex! Once we started communicating our solution to our TARGET MARKET, everything else just fell into place.

An Easy To Reach Market

The second thing you want to look for in a TARGET MARKET is a group that's easy to reach. If you say you want owners of one legged dogs, we can find owners of one legged dogs, but it's really kind of hard to find owners of one legged dogs. So you want to make sure that you've got a group that's

FreshStart

Telephone

WHAT: Provides local, long distance and cellular telephone service.

WHO: Credit challenged,

big enough to have their own media such as magazines, television shows or blogs. With the OB/GYN doctor, for example, there are women magazines that target women over 35. There are local groups for women over 35. There are online networking meet up groups. There's media so that we can reach them. The perfect TARGET MARKET is one big enough to have its own media, but small enough that the big corporations don't focus on them.

How I built my telephone company so quickly - For example, when I first started with credit challenged customers, nobody wanted them. The competition threw these customers away. The competition made it difficult for the customer to obtain telephone service after a disconnection. What made FreshStart different? I made it easy for the customer to sign up. Our promotions featured this language, no $500 deposit required, only $100 activation fee for FreshStart telephone service within 48 hours. We guarantee that you'll never get disconnected again. As long as you follow the rules, you'll never have to worry about your phone being disconnected again." It worked great until I got super successful and the big companies were like, "Hey, wait a minute. Oh my gosh! Look! She's charging 2 ½ times what we're charging these same credit challenged customers. How is she doing it?" And then they started to go after my TARGET MARKET, but that's what happens when you get really good, so you have got to constantly evolve which you'll learn in the next chapters. But now that you get the secrets of creating your million dollar business, you are just going to do it again and again which is basically what I did.

A Market That Will Buy

One of the things I like to do is give my TARGET MARKET person a name, so that whenever I'm creating an ad, I do it as if I'm sitting across from her. I knew that my TARGET MARKET was a woman between 28 and 35. She had children. She had a job. She was having problems making ends meet. So I named her Tanisha and every time I wrote an ad, my newsletter, I always wrote it as if I was talking to Tanisha. Once you know the TARGET MARKET and GREAT SOLUTION, it makes everything fall into place!

You need to find a group that has money to pay you. Here's the key question. Who would be most likely to buy your product or service? It is not everybody. It is not all women. It is not all men. It is not all African American people. You need to be able to break these down and define your TARGET MARKET. As we discussed in the introduction, unless you're starting with

$1,000,000, then it is hard to reach EVERYONE, all women, and all men.

MDE RULE #4 – You don't have enough money to reach EVERYBODY. Be specific when picking your TARGET MARKET.

MDE RULE #5 – *Your GREAT SOLUTION must solve your TARGET MARKET's biggest problem.*

Your TARGET MARKET Can Help You Find a GREAT SOLUTION

So here's your test. Does this TARGET MARKET have a problem that needs to be solved? Once you get this piece, then that's going to be your GREAT SOLUTION. So now that you have these two things clearly defined, we are ready to move on!

Chapter 3: MARKETING CALENDAR – How to Schedule Your Income

Use the calendar to build your marketing and how to schedule your money.

Random Marketing Acts Generate Random Money

Most entrepreneurs decide to market when business is slow. This can be a fatal mistake. One of my favorite songs by The Whispers is entitled "You never miss your water until your well runs dry", and it demonstrates this error in judgment. If you are not focused on consistently bringing in a new customer or at least new dollars from existing customers, the business will die.

The beginning of a MARKETING CALENDAR starts with a thorough review of your business. Start looking at when the business should flourish; just like everybody is not your TARGET MARKET, your business is not going to be busy at *all* times. Creating the MARKETING CALENDAR will produce a better and more consistent business, but not the same customer flow.

The biggest idea about a MARKETING CALENDAR to grasp is, you need ways that you can leverage your business by using what is already in your prospect's and your customer's minds. Such as what is going on in the world. So during the holidays, you should either be doing a holiday sale or talking about the New Year, talking about that predisposed deadline because people are ready to make changes in their lives during the holidays. As a consultant, when I go into most businesses, I see that the business owner has one or two things planned for the year and that's it. Then they are just hoping somebody's going to buy from them each day, instead of a real clear strategy. That's what the MARKETING

CALENDAR is used for, planning your strategy.

The Marketing Triangle

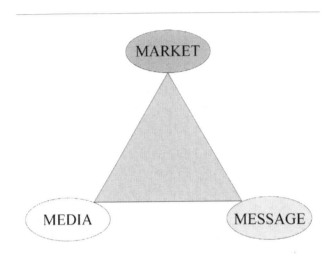

Let me describe how a typical decision happens in

most businesses. In walks a media sales person. Yellow

pages, radio, or billboard, and the sales person begins to

describe the best way to reach customers for your business.

Then as the sales person is giving the presentation, you, the

business owner drift away deep in your mind creating

intricate, detailed mathematic calculations using the "typical

REACH numbers" the sales person presented.

> *This billboard is seen by 492,000 cars every day. What if just 1% called?*

Then it happens – You sign on the dotted line and wait, and wait, and then in 90 days you can't see where you received 49 calls total.

The Reason – You started with the wrong question. The decision to start marketing should never start with the media; it should start with your TARGET MARKET.

So the peak of the triangle is going to be your market. The left side of the triangle is going to be your message and the right side is going to be your media. The last chapter covered the TARGET MARKET. Now that we know who your TARGET MARKET is, what kind of message do they want to hear? What is it? It should be tied to the same message that you are giving for your GREAT SOLUTION. The last thing that you pick is going to be your media, because media should be based on what your TARGET MARKET reads, watches, and listens to.

Let's use my telephone company, FreshStart as an example – My message: To guarantee that you are never going to get your phone disconnected again. My TARGET MARKET: People in Las Vegas who had been disconnected before. Then I could pick my media. Here's the deal, I got super great rates for the newspaper, but my prospects didn't read the newspaper. So whether it was free or not, why would I run ads if my prospects don't read the newspaper? Think of where your clients are. Your media should only be purchased based on if the media reaches your TARGET MARKET and if the GREAT SOLUTION can be conveyed.

MDE Rule #6 – *Random acts of marketing, generates random income.*

Create a Marketing Budget

My theory – a marketing budget is not a percentage of total sales, projected sales, etc, etc, etc. I believe you pick a number, a number that you can invest. Then stick to it, until the marketing media campaign is tested and proven.

MDE Rule #7 – *Never sign a year contract!*

Without proof that the media produces Return On Investment (ROI). No matter how "cheap" it appears.

MDE Rule #8 – *The most expensive marketing, is marketing that didn't work.*

Even if the budget is $100 per month, be consistent with it.

Being consistent is also going to create customers for life. The more people know, like, and trust you, the more they are going to buy from you and the more they feel like they understand you and you understand them. What are you doing to make sure that you are right in front of your prospect when your customer or prospect is ready to buy?

The Crystal Ball Theory

When we're ready for our TARGET MARKET to buy, often times your TARGET MARKET is not ready to buy. Either they have not planned on it, or they don't get paid until next Friday, so we don't know when they are ready to buy. That's what this crystal ball theory is about. Since we don't know when somebody is ready to buy, we have to show up more often and more consistently.

Some business owners get discouraged after completing a marketing campaign because of the response rate, but the problem is they expect homeruns for every campaign instead of consistently executing base hits. Your marketing then builds like a volcano. I never want you to be discouraged if the response to your marketing is not exactly what you want it to be. We are going to keep doing more and more and more and as we do more and more and more, the momentum keeps building and your response gets better. So no matter what, we've got to be there consistently and using various media.

Core of the MARKETING CALENDAR Starts with Developing Your Own Media

The MDE Rule #9 - *The most important media and your first pick needs to be a company newsletter*

<u>Why you need a company newsletter?</u>

1. To communicate consistently with your prospects and customers

2. To create a relationship

3. To stay in your customer's mind

4. To create an ongoing conversation

5. To have a place to publicly acknowledge and thank referrals, share good news, and demonstrate your company's culture

First pick out a marketing theme and then your calendar is based around three things that we need to plan in there. Number one is a newsletter. Number two is a monthly marketing piece. Number three is your social media - your Facebook, blogs, and Twitters. All of these are all connected based on the particular theme of your marketing. It should be connected in your MARKETING CALENDAR.

Your MARKETING CALENDAR helps you plan how you will be consistently communicating with your customers and prospects.

What Should Be In The Newsletter?

MDE Rule #10 – *The goal of your newsletter is consumption, getting it open, read and keeping an ongoing conversation*

Let's start with what should *not* be in the newsletter – BORING INDUSTRY FACTS.

If you are a CPA and enjoy reading the latest tax updates, they should never be included in the newsletter.

Even if most of your clients need to know the information. The newsletter cannot be boring – if it is, it will become less effective.

The first thing that you are going to do is you are going to write down 20 topics about your business. Simply pick 20 things about your business that you can write about. Take those same problems of your TARGET MARKET from chapter 2 and include them as one of 20 things that you are going to have as topics that you can write about for the newsletter.

One of the objections I always get when I suggest doing a newsletter is that people say, "Oh, I don't know what to write about! Nobody wants to hear that much from me!" So here's your equation. 80% of your newsletter is going to be core relationship building (CRB). CRB meaning just random items that you can pick out from either a trivia, a picture, a picture of your children, a picture of your dog, a picture of the weather changing, a new item that you have either in your store, in your office, just something that has absolutely nothing to do with you selling your product or service, but all to do with your personal and company values. Then the other 20% will be related to your industry. 15% related to your industry topic and 5% is the portion where you can sell. You are not going to use your newsletter as a sales mechanism. Here's the reason why: if you only create a newsletter to sell something, people are going to get turned off and they are not going to open the newsletter. They are not going to read it whether you send it online or offline. Because unless the customer is looking for a sale, they will not read it. (Remember the Crystal Ball Theory)

Why do you think soap operas have been so successful for so long? Soap operas worked because they are a continuation of a story. It's got drama. It's got characters. People want to FOLLOW UP with them, read about what is going on. So my particular newsletter that I send has 80% of it about my daughter, about my crazy travel schedule and about fun pictures of my travels, funny things that happened in the airport, my big a-ha moments from my clients and maybe a sale. I hardly ever sell in the newsletter. I sell maybe four times a year and the rest of the time I'm having an ongoing conversation with my TARGET MARKET to make them feel as if they know me – building a relationship.

Even when I send my online newsletters, and awesome comment that I get is, "Wow, Richelle, even when you are selling you still gave me an a-ha moment so that I can go back and take action." The main goal of a newsletter is consumption. You want people to open it and read it. If every time that they open it, "There's 15% off! There's 17% off! There's $5 off!" they are going to go, "Oh, it's just another offer" unless they are ready to buy, the newsletter will not be opened. You want to make sure that you keep nurturing the relationship with those that aren't ready to buy right now and you do that by giving lots of fun information. For examples of newsletters I send for my businesses and private clients, go to www.MDEnation.com to sign up for the MDE Newsletter.

So how do you pick your themes? Write down the dates of industry important events. This is important because you want to use things that are already happening that your customers and prospects are interested in. For example, if you are in the weight loss industry, January's a big month; we know that people decide to make New Year's resolutions. You should have something going on in your MARKETING CALENDAR for January. If you are in finances; we want to make sure that we're talking about how to have financial independence, how to start the year off right. I like to pick a theme every single month so that once you have a specific theme, then you can put it in and work your other marketing pieces around the theme. My private coaching client owns a dance studio, she uses National Dance week in April as a theme.

Write down any other holidays you love. I like to use really crazy holidays. We have a National Root Beer Float Day on August 6th. Every National Root Beer Float Day, for my physician clients, we show up with root beer and ice cream and that's our way of showing appreciation, saying 'Thank You.' Our newsletter is all themed with root beer floats and the funny things that you can do with it, funny things you can add to it to make it taste better or to customize it if you want to use diet ice cream and diet soda. It's just a way to have something else to talk about and a bonding relationship instead of just general business.

One of the challenges that I get with every physician client is they always want to tell me about what they love. My optometrist always wants to write about damages to your eyes and why you should wear sunglasses and nobody wants to hear about that every month. We already know how smart he is and your clients already know how smart you are. That's why they are coming to you. So the newsletter is not about you showing how smart you are about your subject. It's about you being able to show that you are a real person. In my newsletter, I talk about my failures a lot. I talk about how I don't know how to cook, but the one thing I understand is how to build businesses. It gets me on the same level as my clients and they feel empowered by the fact that I'm exposing a bit more of myself.

All Media Bonus - Adding Personality

Whatever you do, you marketing cannot be boring. What personality you are going to add? Are you going to use your kids? If you don't have kids, are you going to use pets? If you don't have a pet, are you going to create a persona or a celebrity? Beyonce says she has Sasha Fierce.

Kids work perfectly because they say funny random things. You've got fabulous pictures of them. I used one with my kid where it was time to do her hair and she's got the biggest afro of all time. I get tons of comments on that one. The picture I have of my kid with the blanket on her head, I love to show that one because people laugh because she thought she was Hannah Montana, Miley Cyrus, so she wore the blanket on her head forever. Add different things, different ways to create personality and to get people talking about what you are doing, which is always fun and ultimately creates a bond.

Online V. Offline Newsletters

If you decide to deliver your newsletter online via email, you have to send it a minimum of once per week or four times per month. If you do offline, then you only have to print and mail it once per month. You can decide. I like to do both. Here's what is great, you can take the basic printed offline newsletter that you would put out in print and break it into four pieces because customers are not going to want to consume that much content online at one time. You want to make sure that they can read through it in about one to three minutes, three minutes tops for online.

Offline newsletters should take them about 5 to 17 minutes to read through, even if it's just a ton of pictures. You want to have lots of pictures and you want it to generate interaction. I want it to look like something that you put together and that's on purpose. If it looks too professional, then it will resemble an ad. The most effective way is to make it appear as if you put it together.

There are tons of newsletter templates online. If you have Microsoft© Word, it is included in your Microsoft© product. Here's another bonus, take the items that you use in your newsletter and repurpose it online in your social media, blogs, Facebook Fan Page, Twitter, or LinkedIn and with anything that you post. What I do is create my newsletter for the month. Then once I have completed it, I take my ideas, my inspiration, the funny things, the pictures of my kids, and I use those same items on my Facebook, on my Twitter, and on my blog, on my LinkedIn profile, so that it's all connected. Now, when somebody gets a print newsletter from me, they may not have seen all of the information but they are giggling because it is a double whammy. They are seeing it online and they are seeing it offline.

Then I break down some of the articles and I put them online too. Most of the time what I do is I write my online article and then I put that as my intro to my print newsletter.

MDE Rule #11 - *Repurpose all content.*

If you can spend two hours a month writing your monthly newsletter, that will take care of everything you need to write for the month because you can break it up and use it all on your social media. The MARKETING CALENDAR answers the question, "What should I post today?" You are going to post what you have already put in your newsletter based on themes in your MARKETING CALENDAR.

Color or Black and White?

Do you send the print newsletter out with color or black and white? I always do black and white. I have sent maybe two newsletters in all of my history in color. Only because printing them in color is expensive. Number two, once you send it in color, you can't go back to black and white. Of course if it's online, your email's going to be in color and the pictures look better. What you can do from your print newsletter is post the color version on your blog so that the customer can come and see what is happening.

The 1st Newsletter

I just want to tell you, your first newsletter is going to be awful. You are going to spend 10 to 15 hours. Let me tell you that I look back at the newsletters that I have done and I go, "Ugh, I had the nerve to send that out. That was terrible!"

Here's the last bonus, your customer doesn't know what it's supposed to look like, so they will not judge you. But it's not about content, it's about consistency. It's not about the content, it's about the consistency. Remember, you do not have a crystal ball and we do not know when people are ready to buy. But if you make sure that when they are ready, they remember you, it will dramatically change your income.

Your consistent communication makes you hard to forget.

MDE Rule #12 – *It's not about the content, it's about the*

consistency.

Chapter 4: FOLLOW UP System – the $ is in the FOLLOW UP

Have You Given Up Too Soon?

Your business gold mine is in the FOLLOW UP. The next step is all about FOLLOW UP. I am breaking it down into the FOLLOW UP for prospects and FOLLOW UP for clients, so that we are going to put together systems, entry points, and what should happen for each. I realized early on in my telephone company that prospects buy after they've investigated. But often, most entrepreneurs give up too soon on prospects. They say, "You know, it wasn't easy. I couldn't convert them. Nobody bought." I love to ask, "Well, how many times did you send a marketing piece out?" "Oh, well I sent it once." I say, "Oh geez. Once? Really?" Seriously? (in my best Kim Kardashian voice)

FOLLOW UP with Prospects

If you only send once, whether it is an email or a direct mail piece or a Facebook post, what you are hoping is that the moons collide. There are a lot of really good lessons in this, but it's not just about persistence, it's about what you are supposed to send out. It is not to hit a hammer over their head. It's about getting the prospect to overcome why they are not buying from you, because there are several reasons why they are not.

Just because somebody does not buy from you immediately, it does not mean that they are not interested. Remember in the last chapter when I told you about having a crystal ball? We never know when a prospect is ready to buy, so we need to create the systems so that we can automatically

FOLLOW UP with everyone. But first let's understand the reasons why people do not buy from you.

Why People Are Not Buying

Lack of Information

One of the reasons people are not buying from you is that there is not enough information available to them about your product or service. They are not sure if the product or service will work for them. They are not sure about you. They have never heard of you before. They are not sure of your company. They are kind of confused about what is going on.

Lack of a GREAT SOLUTION

Another reason they don't buy is that your product or service does not solve their big problem. Remember we talked about making sure that your GREAT SOLUTION resonates with your TARGET MARKET and be able to solve their problem.

Not only do they not believe it, but it's not actually solving their biggest problems.

Lack of a Problem

The prospect will not buy if they are not sure that they have a problem that needs to be solved. Often, the business owner has to show the prospect what you propose to be a problem. Or what their problem really is. For example at my telephone company FreshStart Telephone the real problem was the customer kept getting their service disconnected, it was not about the price of the service.

Lack of Communication

The prospect has not heard from you in a long time. They have forgotten about you. They forgot that you were even available. They can't remember the last time you communicated with them or mailed them anything.

Lack of Attention

People are not buying from you because your company is not in the front of their mind when they are ready to buy. When they want to buy they are focused on another company. They have not heard from you enough to think of your company.

Lack of Ability

Your potential customers may not buy because they were unable to afford your service/product when it was time to buy. Your offer deadlines will result in some customer not being able to buy. However, clearly communicating deadlines in advance helps customers be able to purchase when the offer is available.

Lack of Clarity

Your potential customers won't buy if they thought you sold out. They thought you were not providing the product or service anymore. I watch entrepreneurs all the time. They run from product to product and service to service

- to the next shiny object - because they think that this is a better way to do things. This leads to a situation where the prospect is confused and says, "Really, you still do that?" Do your customers know that you still provide the basic service that you used to provide before?

Lack of Contact

The final reason people do not buy is that your contact information changed. You changed locations, your old numbers were not updated; you have not updated your website so all of your old information is still there. That is why consistent FOLLOW UP is so important. Let your customers know changes in your business. FOLLOW UP is going to help you remove the reasons why people are not buying. Let's get to work on your FOLLOW UP!

The FOLLOW UP Sequence- How to follow up without being obnoxious

The FOLLOW UP sequence is tied to each of your entry points. What are entry points? Entry points are how a new prospect gets to you. How do you meet prospects? What happens after you meet them?

Entry Point: Belly to Belly

Belly to belly; that means that you have met the prospect in person, such as at an event. Inevitably when you are at a networking event, you are going to meet somebody who says, "Will you send me some more information? I would love to hear more about your product or service." What I see happen, is that business owners return from the event with a stack of cards and normally they are set on the desk. Maybe they are in the bottom of your purse. Maybe they are still in the bottom of that free bag that you got from the event. Instead of everybody getting the same response, the business owner starts going through the cards and testing their memory.

"Was he nice? He was really cute. I think they were really interested." Instead of having a formalized system where everybody gets the exact same, FOLLOW UP messages.

Your FOLLOW UP sequence should lead to nurturing relationships. We tend it like it is a garden. We are going water it, feed it, just like we do an expensive crop, we nurture them. How does this happen for every card I receive...First, I send a thank you card. Second, send an overview about your product or service to them in the mail. Then the last email communication is an offer to meet with them.

    a. Thank you card

    b. Send an overview

    c. Email an offer to meet

Very simple, I know, but what happens is entrepreneurs don't do it all the time. If you did it all the time, then you would have prospects consistently flowing through your marketing and sales funnel. Unfortunately, you pick and choose which ones you want to FOLLOW UP with instead of everyone entering the same system. The overview about your business will also answer typical objections that the prospect might have. We answer these questions that we have discussed already in the GREAT SOLUTION chapter. Make sure to include all the detail that is needed to make a buying decision about your product.

After the email offer to meet, whether they have met with you or not, now we are going to send them our monthly print newsletter, to be there when the prospect might be ready.

Entry Point: REFERRAL - Referral FOLLOW UP

This entry point FOLLOW UP begins with an email introduction. Here is the template, "Hi (Name), [Brad, the person who referred me] suggested that we meet. I know that is kind of confusing, but I'm also sending you some basic information about me and my product or service in the mail." Let me know if there's anything that I can help you with immediately." Step 2 - Send a thank you note to the person who referred you. "Thank you so much for thinking of me. I can't wait to help [Brad] with his business." Step 3 - Mail that same overview that we created for the belly to belly to the new referred person.

Step 4 - Send the referral an email and offer to meet. Then everybody, both the person who referred you and the new referee are going to be added on to your monthly print newsletter. Simple process, but effective, if completed each time you receive a new referral.

MDE Rule #13 – Every *prospect receives a FOLLOW UP sequence which leads to the monthly newsletter.*

Entry Points - Website

Your website should capture leads for your business or sell a product or service. Most websites are full of information that can be found on the company brochure.

Capturing information from the traffic that arrives at your website is essential. Currently there is not a software program that will give the business owner contact information for people who visit your website. Generic numbers such as numbers of visitors, length of time on site, pages viewed, all valuable information, however not enough to generate revenue.

The MDE way of generating revenue from your website is to have two main focuses: Lead Capture and Immediate Sales

1. <u>Lead Capture Bait</u> – Who wants to sign up for another newsletter? But on my site, I offer a free copy of my first book *"How to Build a Million Dollar Business in Las Vegas Without the Casinos"* in exchange for the prospects email and contact information.

   a. Good examples of Lead Capture Bait: (Ways to exchange something of value for the prospects contact information)
      i. Free industry survey
      ii. Free book
      iii. Free white paper
      iv. Free report
      v. Free discount coupon

vi. Free appetizer

2. <u>Sell Product or Service</u> – Have clear information. Recognizing the problems of the TARGET MARKET and highlighting the GREAT SOLUTION.

Now this is where it gets a little complicated and will probably take you the longest amount of time. It is essential to create entry points on your website. The entry point is going to be an offer for something for free. This can be a product or perhaps a report on the seven common mistakes in your industry.

1. Capture lead
2. Deliver free offer
3. Add to newsletter

How to Automate the FOLLOW UP System

I use Infusionsoft.com for my website lead capture FOLLOW UP campaigns. The system will do the FOLLOW

UP, using automatic responders based on the information entered, links clicked or pages visited.

I use SendOutCards.com for direct mail. I absolutely love SendOutCards.com because you can create FOLLOW UP campaigns in them. You can create a welcome campaign that will include a gift, a thank you, a card to FOLLOW UP with them, a postcard reminder, anything you want. For a retail account, it is free to sign up. Of course, for full disclosure, all of these products are affiliate programs for me. I believe and use each of them, it is not just about making money.

Systems for each entry point will build your business quicker because your competition is not doing it. Your competition gives up. Your competition stops. This FOLLOW UP is what took my business from $100,000 to $1 million. It was implementing the FOLLOW UP system to convert every single prospect that comes through while never ever giving up or quitting. Several popular email programs will create automatic FOLLOW UP such as iContact.com,

ConstantContact.com and aWeber.com. They also come with

lead capture forms to put leads into your database

automatically from your website.

MDE Rule #14 – *Your website must be capturing leads.*

Chapter 5: Retention – Love the One You're With: 3 Simple Steps

Imagine if every customer that you ever had was still paying you. Would your business look different? It all starts with properly taking care of your customers and directing their steps to stay, buy more and refer. How does it work?

Step One – Your Wowing Welcome

Keeping customers starts before the sale but amplifies after the exchange of money.

Your "Wowing Welcome" occurs after the customer makes a purchase. So many times customers do not know what the next step is in your business. They do not know what they are supposed to do and it is up to you to tell them what their next step should be. You also want to properly thank them, with the size of the gift based on how much the customer invested with you! I will discuss more on thanking them in a moment. This is your opportunity to provide information, reducing customer service calls.

I like to include in the welcome letter how to do business with me. For example, for all of my private doctor clients, we send their new patients the office hours. We include information on how to get prescriptions refilled; best times to call the office; and how to schedule an appointment. The patient is not sure how best to do business with you. I know that you think that they should know it automatically, but they really do not know unless you tell them.

You need a Wowing Welcome system. Your customer should say, "Oh wow!" after each interaction with your company. Not "Oh no!" It should be something that they are going to tell their friends about. Your welcome letter helps expand and seal the new relationship. Best of all, it will eliminate buyer's remorse. Additional benefits can include an up-sell and ask for referrals.

Benefits of a WOWing Welcome Sequence for RETENTION

Benefit #1 Remove Remorse

If your GREAT SOLUTION is about guaranteeing financial independence for a single mom, then they better get something that talks about what they need to do right now to start securing their independence. If you tell the prospect, "I'm going to save your marriage" and that is the reason why they purchased, when your business welcome letter arrives, it better say something about the 'Five tips of how we are going to save your marriage.' The welcome letter helps to manage their expectations plus eliminate returns.

Benefit #2 The Up-sell

Turn your welcome letter into additional sales by adding an up-sell opportunity. You've experienced it before from Amazon.com ™ - "People who bought this book also bought this book." Up-sell the customer into your next product or service. This is going to expands your current customer from a $10 to a $100 customer. Amazon.com has mastered this simple technique into additional millions!

One of the deterrents to retention of FreshStart telephone customers is that the payment plan was difficult to stick to. The payments were due on the first. Payments were late on the third and on the sixth of the month, if payment was not recorded, service was disconnected. In my welcome letter, I detailed out about our payment plan and about how I wanted to make sure the customer understood why this payment plan was actually good for them. I explained how to avoid the late fee. The welcome letter helped to disclose items that may seem tricky.

Benefit #3 - Request Referrals

Use this opportunity to ask for referrals. I add a line in my welcome letter, it reads, "My vision is helping 1 million business owners create million dollar businesses. If you know of anyone who could use my help, please send them to grab my first book, "How to Build a Million Dollar Business in Las Vegas Without the Casinos" for free here – www.TheMillionDollarEquation.com . These benefits of the WOWing Welcome Letter quadrupled my RETENTION rate.

Step Two – Thank Your Buyer

Using thank you cards or gifts helps the customer know their business is appreciated. Studies show that 84% of the customers leave your business because they don't think you care. Devise a way to properly thank the buyer. MDE Rule of Thumb - 10% of the sales should be spent on gifts. You may send the gifts a couple of times a year or all in one gift. Being cheap is a sure way to lose a valuable customer.

When I bought my second house, the realtor I used was the same one who I bought two rental properties with. And when I upgraded to the new 4,000 sq. ft., 5 bedroom, 4 bath, pool, Jacuzzi, RV parking house, my thank you was a jar filled with colored pasta. Total $10.00. I'm still telling the story about her, but now in a good way. I realize there are some legal restrictions of gifts. But closer to the $50.00 limit would've been nice.

MDE Rule #15 – *Let the customer know you care consistently.*

Step Three – Your Monthly Newsletter: To keep customers connected, a monthly newsletter will keep them in the loop

The first step in retaining your clients is staying in front of them with your monthly newsletter. Remember all the excuses that people use for not buying from you in the last chapter? Your newsletter helps remove those excuses for your clients so they can keep buying from you. The monthly

newsletter should educate about other products or services. It

should also build a community for customers. The newsletter

is not to tell the customer how smart you are or how much

you know about your industry. It should build a relationship.

Step Four – Send Birthday/Anniversary Cards

Not only properly thanking customers, but showing up

when they least expect it. Birthdays are important in your

customer's lives. Anniversary cards and discounts are great

too! To expand on the anniversary idea, I send "Happy

Anniversary" of their first appointment, 1st sale, and 1st house

just to make it fun!

Chapter 6: Reactivation

Baby Come Back – Now's the Time to Make Quick Money

The easiest customer for you to sell is your existing customer. The second easiest customer is a reactivated customer, a customer who used to be with you, who now needs to come back and buy from you again. Reactivation is how to create a cash flow surge in your business by winning back old clients.

Cracks in Your Foundation

Before we get into how you can build a reactivation strategy, let me talk about the cracks in your foundation. Often, as soon as I go into a new consulting client, I will start with a reactivation campaign. Obviously the client always wants me to start with this one too. The challenge is they are not always ready because there are tons of cracks in the foundation. Are there are cracks in your foundation? What do I mean by cracks in the foundation?

Let's start with not properly thanking or not properly following up. The cracks are all the systems that we have been exposing in the previous chapters. Communicating the GREAT SOLUTION; solving a big problem; knowing who your defined TARGET MARKET is; having the correct message; making sure there is a welcome letter; are we properly thanking them; and really nurturing each customer is this happening in your business? Once these are working we are able to send out a reactivation campaign and get sales quickly. But you can't have any cracks in your FOUNDATION.

You probably are able to give me a whole bunch of reasons why past customers leave or stop using your products or services. Is it because they no longer feel connected? Has your price changed? Have they forgotten you exist? Have you stopped giving them fantastic experience and value? Have they outgrown your current offerings? Have you stopped solving their big problem? Do you have a customer service problem? Now, what have you changed in your business to address the challenges?

The Importance of Reactivation

Why is reactivation so important? Almost 90% of customers leave you because...? They leave because of indifference. They feel like you do not give a hoot. Lazy entrepreneurs only sell price but not experience. Here is the other reason why reactivation is so important, because the new provider is not paying attention to them either. Wherever the customer went, the new company is not doing a good job either. So you have the opportunity and the ability to win the customer back. It is important, so let's move on to the timing of a reactivation campaign.

Reactivation In Your MARKETING CALENDAR

I like to put a reactivation strategy in when I create my MARKETING CALENDAR. Normally I do my reactivation in January or September. January is a great time for a new start to a new year. September is when kids go back to school and customers are back from vacations and ready to buy. FreshStart customers liked to buy in January and September.

Holidays are a great time to focus on reactivating old clients. I have a now famous reactivation campaign for FreshStart during Halloween entitled "What Was Scaring Me?"

For a copy of the entire campaign, go to

http://www.MDENation.com/Reactivation

How did I get the idea? I read in the local newspaper about two kids who were playing in their parent's closet and found a gun. Tragically, one of the kids shot the other one. Even worse, it took an extra 15 minutes for emergency response to get to the children because the family did not have a phone in their house. This story became my theme for reactivation. I sent the campaign to

> "I realized maybe I didn't say thanks enough and I am really embarrassed, but I would love to have your business back and I am giving you a cool discount"

people who had been disconnected, with the headline "You know what is really scaring me? Halloween is okay, but what is really scaring me is that you have children in your home, but you have no phone. We would love to have you back".

The Thanksgiving holiday works perfectly too. Here's the theme to use. One of my private clients sent his reactivation letter all based around their annual food drive.

This was a way that he could get back chiropractic patients who had not seen him in a while. The campaign theme, "Bring in a can of food and I will do an adjustment for you for free because we want to make sure that we are able to collect as much food for charity as we can."

Reactivation Time Triggers

There should be an alarm that activates when it is time for your customer to purchase again. At FreshStart, it was easy because we disconnected

FRESHSTART REACTIVATION CAMPAIGN

It was a "Get Out of Jail Free" card that I customized from the Monopoly game. The letter headline, "I don't know what happened", even though I did know what happened, the customer did not pay their bill. I said, "Maybe it was what we did" because you always want to put the fault on you and it is never on the customer. In reality, they did not pay any of their bills. But if I told them that in the letter, why would they come back? So I told them, "Look, I realize that things change. I realize that bad things happen to good people and sometimes you are unable to pay your bill. What is most important to me is I want you to be able to have a phone in your house. So here is a special discount deal". What was most important to me was not to get their activation or the balance of the outstanding bill; it was to get them back on monthly continuity because that is where I made the most money, and made sure there was a phone in their home.

89

customers every month. Every 90 days, I implemented a reactivation campaign to recover all of the disconnected customers over the last 90 days. Here is what is so exciting. I sent it to 15% the same customers every 90 days and the customer would reconnect for two months and then they would disconnect for two months. Then they would reconnect using the same FOLLOW UP/REACTIVATION campaign. I never changed it.

The Reactivation Campaign

Okay, let's talk about the basics of your campaign. A campaign consists of a certain number of steps to contact a previous customer. We already talked about picking the time in your MARKETING CALENDAR to do a campaign. Now we need to create a campaign.

Steps to complete a Reactivation Campaign
1. *Indentify the list on inactive customers*
2. *Pick the theme of the campaign*
3. *Determine the various media pieces*

4. Determine the delivery schedule

5. Implement the campaign per the delivery schedule

Sample Media Campaign:

	Media	Title	When
Step 1:	Email	Watch Your Mail for the Red Envelope	Day 1
Step 2:	Letter (Red Envelope)	We Want You Back 50% OFF	Day 2
Step 3:	Email	The 50% OFF Expires in 7 Days	Day 4
Step 4:	Postcard	Only 3 Days to Take Advantage	Day 7
Step 5:	Email	It Ends Tonight	Day 9

The most successful REACTIVATION campaigns use multiple-media in the campaign. Don't simply rely on one media. You have to do online, offline and social media. I recently finished another reactivation campaign; it is the end of the year launch for my international mastermind group. Instead of only using direct mail and email, we actually called them to FOLLOW UP. You want to put all of these steps into your campaigns, especially with reactivation. Mail, email, tweet, call, and fax. Use any and all customer contact information.

Don't Forget These Ways to Deliver the Reactivation Message

The easiest way to notify previous customers is to insert the message in your existing media. If you are consistently sending out a newsletter, online or offline, you can put the promotion in your newsletter. A private dentist client of mine didn't have any extra money to spend on a reactivation campaign. But we were already sending a newsletter for him, so I separated his list. I split it into patients that we have seen over the last year and patients that we have not seen during the last year. Each list got a separate newsletter. The patients that we have not seen got a newsletter that was all focused on the reactivation. I just changed out one page from the normal newsletter and put in a page that included all of his discounts, all of the new offers, and a way to reactivate them. That is something that you can

do today.

MDE Rule #16 - *Be sure to get your list right first.*

MDE Rule #17 - *Make your budget so that you know how much you can spend and you can make the decision on what media you are going to use.*

People should be on your list even if they have not

purchased from you in five years. Never take inactive

customers off your list.

Drafting the Reactivation Campaign

Your offer has got to be better than normal. So if you

always give free shipping or free poster or 5 dollars off, then

this deal has to be different to reactivate a former customer.

It can't be the standard offer. This is what I have found from

experience, if I am always sending the same offer, then my

former clients did not feel special. As soon as I changed the

offer to one that was a little bit more then they came in droves.

At FreshStart instead of just coming in and getting a free cell

phone accessory, now I included the free charger, the free
accessory, and a free month of service, then the customer
returned.

MDE Rule #18 - *Make sure that when you create your offer
for reactivation that it is better than*

your normal offer.

Add Your Social Proof

Add testimonials to the marketing pieces.

Reactivation Headline & Guarantee to Use in the Media

Your headline should acknowledge that the customer is
lost. Then your guarantee should be equally powerful. You
want to get them back!

Take full responsibility for the customer being lost.
Sample, "We have not kept up with you." Acknowledge this
is a great offer, " I know that this is a really crazy offer and if I
would have given you this before, you probably wouldn't have
left, but now I realize my mistake is and I'd love for you to
come back."

Then mention any other changes since they left and why it is easier to do business with you now. Write down what you have done to fix the previous problems or cracks in your foundation. Include, "You know what? I realize one of the reasons why you disconnected service might be because you didn't really understand what day your bill is due. Here's what changed, FreshStart now, has three FOLLOW UPs that we send to you, plus we make it fun for you so that you'll never forget and never get disconnected again." You see, once again, we have taken this off the customer and put it on us.

Chapter 7: Referrals

Evangelize Your Customers to Become Your Sales Force

Let's review my Three R's…retention, reactivation, and referrals! This chapter on Referrals will focus on how to double your clients immediately. If you have three, let's go get six. If you have 300, let's go get 600. It starts with making sure that you have the strategies in place.

When I meet people at networking events and they find out I am a marketing expert then they always want to say to me, "Oh, well I don't have to do any marketing. My customers just come automatically to me, word of mouth" like it is a sin to invest in your business. I giggle and smile and go,

"Oh great! So how are you getting the word of mouth to work?" Basically, I'm asking how do you get referrals? The response is a blank stare. Imagine if each one of your customers referred another one to your business would your cashflow be different? Just so we are very clear, your only job in life once you get a customer is to keep them and to get them to tell somebody else about your service.

MDE Rule #19 - *Your one and only goal. Keep the customers and get them to tell somebody else.*

If you are not achieving that goal and you do not have systems designed to reach it, you are wasting your time. You remember the old Clairol™ commercial where she told two friends and each of those told two friends and then so on? Your business multiplied by the power of referrals grows very quickly. The one thing that I did at FreshStart, my telephone company, is that I was able to grow quickly because of this referral system. Not only did I have cool marketing stuff, but

I made sure that I was grooming and conditioning each new customer so that they were telling their friends.

The 7 Step Referral System

The seven step system creates a predictable, measurable, duplicatable way to generate referrals. The first thing is track, second is earn, then ask, then encourage and reward, then thank, then acknowledge and number seven is Equip and Arm. Let's go over each step one by one. Ready?

7 STEP Referral System

1. *Track*
2. *Earn*
3. *Ask*
4. *Thank*
5. *Acknowledge*
6. *Encourage*
7. *Equip and Arm*

Tracking Your Referrals

Tracking is essential and is the trigger for other systems to begin, so don't skip this step. Once again, when I ask business owners about how are they are getting word of mouth referrals and new customers, they have absolutely no idea. They have no idea who referred them or it is happening so rarely that they can't help but know who all of their referring customers are.

With my private clients, we create a tracking system. What systems are in place for you to track your referrals? Do you have forms? Do you have contact management software? Or do you have 3x5 cards? All of those things work. It is very important that you are tracking them in one way or another.

Here is an example from one of my private clients; he is a dentist specializing in Periodontics. We created this form for him and on it we have the patient information, including date of birth; that is important because we send birthday cards to all of his patients. We require their address, their city, their state. There is a place for email. We have a 'Where did you hear about us?' box to track the name of a referring doctor or friend.

Anzalone Periodontics

1606 Royal Avenue
Monroe, LA 71201
Phone (318) 998-3027

Patient Information

Name: _____   Birth Date: _____

Address: _____

City: _____   State: _____   Zip: _____

Phone: _____   Email: _____

How did you hear about Anzalone Periodontics?

____ Internet   ____ Postcard   ____ Public Speaking

____ Insurance   ____ TV Show

Referring Doctor (Name): _____

Referring Friend (Name): _____

Other: _____

Signature: _____   Date: _____

I understand that this information will be used for tracking purposes as well as to communicate with
me about medical and non-medical issues. I understand that this medical practice sends direct mail,
emails and calls to communicate with its patients.

What happens after a patient completes the form? Enter them into our database. We track the referring doctor because we give gifts based on the referrals. The one thing that you need to learn is to make sure that you are not only tracking, but that you are tracking accurately and that you know what to do with the tracking.

Some additional ideas:

Send "Thank You's" to each new patient

Send "Happy Birthday" cards during their birthday month

Earn the Referral

The second piece of the referral system is to earn. Are you delivering the best product or service? Is every experience with you a WOW experience? What type of WOW experiences are you delivering? Establish unparalleled levels of trust and credibility. Give the customer blow away service.

Exceed their expectations. I try to, no matter what, always over deliver so the client is feeling great about being in my program. Exceed their expectations; make them feel like they are the only customer that you have. It is important that your employees feel the exact same way and are delivering that same type of service, whether it be your servers in the café or the people taking their order, from start to finish they have got to feel as if the customer is the most important thing.

Now, activate the law of reciprocity. What happens with the law of reciprocity is that if you keep giving to the customer, the customer will feel as though they should give back to you. They feel comfortable about referring if you have been giving to them. If you deliver a WOW and a spectacular experience, they can't wait to refer. Make sure that you are earning at every opportunity.

Asking for a Referral

Let's get to asking. Are you taking advantage of the moment of truth? The first thing is that you need to establish the expectation and the climate for the referrals right up front with new customers. Clearly ask, saying, "You know what? We grow our business through referrals. We do not do a lot of outside advertising. We would love for you to talk about us to your friends and family and we would love to take care of them." One of the things that we did with my optometrist is when the mother of a family would come in, we made sure that we talked to her about the whole family coming in, since usually it is the mother scheduling the appointments for everyone. Now instead of getting one patient, now we have scheduled the entire family and we have tripled our sales by asking a very important question.

Look at moments to capitalize on. For example, ask verbally in newsletters and in standalone correspondence. How we ask in our newsletter is we spotlight our clients who are already referring. Once we do that, other people say "Well, I want to be spotlighted" and they understand that this is the culture of our business and they refer. If somebody says something great to you, then here is the language that I want you to say back to them. "Thank you for noticing. What are some of the things that we can do together to let the people who work with you, the people in your neighborhood, or others know how they can also come and enjoy?" If you and your staff are consistently asking, you will receive a consistent amount of referrals.

You are entering the conversation with this simple question. Don't get caught up only asking for one - What is funny if you ask for one, you'll only receive one, but if you ask them for ten, they will give you ten. Ask, "And who else comes to mind? Help the customer think of people in specific situations or categories. This is the exact thing that I teach my doctors to do when a patient says, "Oh Doc, this was the most painless procedure ever." The doctor then says, "Oh, thank you so much for noticing. I have spent years making sure that I could provide painless dentistry. What can we do together to make sure that all of your family comes here?"

MDE Rule #20 - *Look for moments of truth to ask for*

referrals

Thanking Referrals

Make sure each client that referred someone to you feels special. It is so important to properly thank your referrals. A coaching client told me there was someone who keeps sending referrals to them. I ask how they are thanking that person. I got a blank stare. I respond, "Oh that means that you are not doing anything?" In some industries, there are some regulations as to how much you can gift someone, but there is always a way. What are you doing? Are you sending a handwritten card to say thank you for the referral? Whether it is a referral partner or a client customer, you need to have something. I love gifts and discounts to both encourage and thank referrals.

One of the things that we did for my optometrist is because he has a retail side of the business; we created special shopping days. Those people who referred him, received an additional discount shopping day. You can do this in every business. You can set up a free time for referring clients to come to the next event, award days, nights to shop, different things so that you are properly thanking them. You can take them all to a sporting game. Get the customer's attention by being creative.

Acknowledge the Referrals

Simply put acknowledge the person who referred. Make sure they know, that you know. I like to acknowledge them inside my newsletter. Use our own media, can include a section where you are thanking people for their referrals. "Thank you so much. I really appreciate it." You can do a drawing. If you have a store and there are a lot of people referring people over, you can put their pictures on the walls. One of the things that I did in my FreshStart office is that I had pictures of people who referred to us up on the wall. They were 8 ½ by 11. We would take a cute picture of them and my customers would bring in their friends and family to see their picture on our wall. They felt famous. They felt fantastic.

Once we took the picture and we put it in our newsletter, we sent them a copy of the picture and the newsletter to the customer, so that most put the picture on their wall a constant reminder of the referral. We went to the dollar store and bought a frame for them so that they could put it on their wall. My grandmother had this rule. Do not give me pictures of the grandkids unless it is in a frame. If you are going to give somebody a picture, make sure that you put it in a frame. And if you give it to them in a frame, they will make a spot for the picture. Adding a great conversation starter for their friends and family.

Encourage and Reward Referrals

We have covered how your system should track, earn, and ask. The next one is how to encourage. What are you doing to encourage people to refer? Of course creating a WOW experience, acting as if this is the way everybody at your company does it. But encouraging them to refer is saying, "You know what, what would really be important to me is if you could have your friends and their families come to the business." One of the things that are in my welcome letter says "Hey, do you know anybody else who could benefit from using The Million Dollar Equation?"

'Do you reward the referral other than just a thank you if the referral doesn't buy?' Yes, I think that you do reward them. Maybe you give them a lesser gift than you would if they actually invested in your product or service, but I definitely like to reward everybody for thinking of me, because I want to keep them encouraged and keep them referring over and over again even if the deal did not materialize.

Perhaps someone has been referred to you and they have not bought from you yet, I see that as an opportunity for you to overwhelm them with your WOW experience. Even though they have not purchased, stay in front of the prospect by sending them your newsletter, every month. There are people who have responded yes for an RSVP to a local event of mine who have never ever shown up, but because I have their name and address, I mail them my newsletter each month. One of my best coaching clients was on my newsletter list for 18 months before he invested. My mentor recommends BUY or DIE is the only way off the prospect list.

Here are some of the rewards that we use for referring. Dinner for two, movie passes, and even gift certificates. Great gifts include a night's stay at a special hotel, box of chocolates, pampering at a salon, a car wash, gift certificates, weekend for two in Las Vegas, San Diego, or some other desirable location. These are the gifts that make customers excited to refer.

Equip and Arm Your Soldiers

Below is the advanced strategy that I stumbled upon at FreshStart. Give the customer the proper tools to overcome their friends and family's objections. First, we start with giving the customer specific language to use to "Win the Argument" with the friends and family.

We prepared each customer with the proper language to overcome if their friends were saying, "Why are you with that stupid little telephone company?" Here was the response : "Well, because they give me gifts every time I pay my bill. Who's giving you gifts when you pay your bill?"

Second, create specific media such as flyers or brochures to help with the convincing and finally, we used old fashioned bribery. The referring customer received a bonus and the new customer received a bonus. At that point, the customer was properly armed.

Chapter 9: 85 Ways to Get a New Customer

The One Way Holding You Back

I am going to tell you the truth, the main thing keeping you from any goal that you have in life is you I bet you know exactly what you should be doing. 90% of the time, you know exactly what it is, but you have chosen to do a workaround, to do something else. For example, public speaking, I hear clients complain all the time. Normally when a private coaching client starts with me and they say, "Okay, Richelle, I want to build my business very quickly." I respond, "Well, the fastest way to build a business is to go out and speak." They fall over themselves. "Oh my, I can't imagine speaking!

I can't do this. I can't do that." I say, "Okay. Then do you want to build your business quickly or not?"

Here is my favorite thing to say to business owners. The one thing that makes you super uncomfortable in your business right now is probably the one thing that is going to catapult you to the next level. You have been avoiding it for however long that you have been in your business. The thing that you are not doing in your business right now is the thing that is really going to catapult you, but just in case you need another 85 things to do, let's work on those next.

The 85 Ways

So how did I come up with the 85 things? Well, it is all based on a story. I was reading a book while I was trying to grow my telephone company. I was frustrated about what was going on and I read about a chiropractor who said he knew that he needed 72 new patients a month in order to reach the million dollar level. I thought I need 85 new customers a month to reach a million dollars within two years. His next sentence was, "I don't know one sure way to get 72 new patients, but I know 72 ways to get one." I thought, "Oh my gosh! Well then I guess I have got to do more."

When you are building your business and trying to do it as efficiently it causes business owners to implement one tactic at a time. But I discovered you have to do a whole lot of things at one time. It can't be one thing. It is about growing and implementing simultaneously instead of sequentially. Most businesses owners complete one tactic and then do that until it stops working and then complete another tactic and do that until it stops, instead of doing ten tactics simultaneously.

One of the fastest media that I have found to grow my business was a radio ad. My customers at FreshStart telephone, did not like to read the newspaper, so I could not advertise in the newspaper. My prospects watched television, but I did not have TV ad money. It was way too expensive to produce and buy a commercial. So I went to our local radio station. I knew that my customers listened to the radio. It was a brand new station that had recently started and they were looking for sponsors. They were offering deeply discounted ads and I got the cheapest ads that I could with them and the station produced my commercial for free, which is what most of them do.

The radio ad generated 400 new calls a month. Now what is so great about it is that remember, because I have my FOLLOW UP system all I needed was the leads because my system worked automatically to convert customers. Once the prospect called, we'd tell them "I'm not sure if we provide service in your area. Can you give us your name and phone number and your mailing address?" Now I had a way to FOLLOW UP with them after they called in. This was going so well that I got lazy on doing the other things. I wanted to focus on this radio ad because they were converting faster than anything else.

Until my competitor bought ads on the same radio station, my leads from the radio station went from 400 to 40 in 30 days! It could have put me out of business if I did not have these other 84 ways to get a new customer. The lesson to learn is diversity leads to stability. Diversity in your marketing will lead to stability in your business.

Vegas Slot Machine Method

Marketing is about return on investment. What normally happens is that you will send out a postcard and only two people respond and you will say, "Alright, I'm not going to do that again." Because you expect all marketing to be winners as soon as you send it out. You expect for the response to be overwhelming no matter what you send out. But, you are looking at the wrong report. Instead of reviewing how many customers, you should review how many dollars.

What I want you to look at is your return on investment. How much did it cost you to send out the media and how much were the sales? Did you make more than it cost to send it out? If you made money, then, it's a winner, we can do it again! So if it cost you $200 to send it out and you received $800 in sales, then you have a 4 to 1 return, because you made four times the amount of your investment.

Then we make a decision on if we should do this again.

With the Las Vegas Slot Machine Method, we want to have 85 of those tactics (machines) generating results or sales, but I know 85 of those are overwhelming, so let's focus on getting ten of them that are producing a 2 to 1 response for you. Meaning there are 10 ways that you are getting two times more than the cost of the marketing. If it cost you $100 to send it out, you get $200 in sales back. If it cost you $1,000 to send it out, you get $2,000, then your income and business building becomes simply a math problem. Find out ten of those things which generate 3 to 1.

You absolutely need a tracking form. You need to know how much it costs you to implement the marketing strategy. If you do not know that, then it is going to be hard for us to determine if this is a valid method for you. Get custom numbers – you have the wonderful Google voice numbers that are free. Assign a certain coupon code to individual telephone numbers.

MDE Rule #21: *Tracking and results dictate if marketing is done again*

Make sure that you understand that tracking is the biggest indicator that we have because once we have the information and we can make accurate decisions to pull the trigger and you invest $500. If you have a 3 to 1 ROI, when you spend $500, you know you are going to get back $1,500. At that point, you have every confidence in the world that if you spend $10,000 that you will make $30,000 – same ratio.

Let's go back to some fundamentals too that is your message, market, and media. Make sure that you have got the target audience right - we never want to forget that part. Let's go through the 85 ways I used to build FreshStart.

1. **Inbound Telemarketing:** Inbound telemarketing is not solely answering calls; it is a calculated script focusing on closing each caller, then leading to a series of up-sells.

2. **Sponsor of Team:** We sponsored a little football team, because our customers loved to have their children involved in outside activities.

3. **Friendly Neighbor Mailing:** It is like a 'welcome to the neighborhood' to new buyers. It is a great way to go in to find brand new people in your neighborhood who do not even know that you are there yet.

4. **Networking Groups**

5. **Walk-In Takeaway:** This is when people come into your store or your location; there is something that they can take with them, a brochure, a handout, a flyer.

6. **After Sale Survey:** The easiest way to get referrals.

7. **Website Widget:** Something on your website so that you are interacting with prospects or customers. At FreshStart, our widget 'Check to see if the service is available in your area' the widget requires the prospects to give us their name and address. Now we were armed with information to FOLLOW UP. By the way, we provided service in every place here in Nevada; however, we used our widget to collect information. The widget always replied 'yes.' .

8. **Search Engine Advertising – Google, Bing & Yahoo "Ad-Words":** Buy "traffic" direct to your website.

9. **Yahoo / Answers:** Post answers to problems.

10. **Car Dealerships:** Look for places where people need your services. (partnerships)

11. **Phonebook:** Look for off subject places or other keywords.

12. **Specialized Phonebooks**: Here you can find different community niches.

13. **Press Releases:** There are free online ones as well as to our local news stations, our community papers, our regular newspapers.

14. **Referral gifts:** Create a way to entice customers to send referrals.

15. **Inactive campaign:** A campaign that reactivates people who have used your service or your product that you have not talked to in a long time.

16. **Unconverted leads campaign**: People who raised their hands and said they are interested in you, but they have never purchased from you. Here is a bonus to this unconverted leads is you can do partnerships with other people and buy their unconverted leads.

17. **Free recorded message:** I love to put in a free recorded message. The message says, "Hey, thank you so much for calling _____. Please tell us your name and address and we will send you back our free report." It is a way to capture their name and to get

them to raise their hand and say, "You know what, I do want more information about your service, but I'm really not ready to buy yet".

18. **Specific Recorded Messages for Different Groups:** We had a free recorded message that was in Spanish

19. **Outside Signage:** A lot of times people can't find you because the signage is not there.

20. **Winner's Wall:** Remember every single month when the customer came to pay their bill, we would do some type of promotion, spin the wheel, and roll the dice. If they won a free month of service, we would take a picture of them and put them on the wall. This actually brought me new customers because they would say, "Oh, what a cute picture of me! Ooh, I'm up on their wall!" and they would bring their friends. When their friends would come in to see the picture, we had a perfect opportunity to sell.

21. **Closing After Buy Referral Coupons:** When we close the customer, before they left our office, we would talk to them and we would go over their contract. Then ask for referrals and we would give them a coupon right then and there to give to their family and their friends.

22. **Move – Thank You & Request for Referral:** When a customer moved to a new location we created a move campaign with gift.

23. **Current Customer Birthday:** Send a birthday card.

24. **Charity Donations / Scholarships**

25. **Seminars:** I am always speaking somewhere. Look for groups in your TARGET MARKET.

26. **Reconnect Notices to the Same Program:** This is another reactivation before we totally disconnected a customer.

27. **Payment Receipts:** at the bottom of the receipts was an offer.

28. **Signage in Store:** You need to have signs in your store.

29. **Thank You Gifts:** When people buy.

30. **Welcome Letters:** See RETENTION.

31. **Reminder Calls:** When we call people about their invoices due, we never said 'Your invoice is due'; we said, "Hey, Thursday is the last day to spin the wheel, roll the dice," and bring a friend.

32. **Voice Broadcast:** There are specific laws in the United States about sending out a voice broadcast, it is an automated message that goes out to the phone and it leaves a voicemail. Automated messages worked really great for us. We would call them and say, "Friday's the last day."

33. **Late Notice Coupons:** Past due notices.

34. **Monthly promotion**: I would throw an event every single month if I could. I mean, it works so well in getting new people to your list and getting new people

interested in what you do so that you can cultivate them and build them.

35. **Radio:** Buy spots.

36. **Radio Show:** Buy show – "Pay for Play" – a local station here provided all technical support. The show cost $600 per month.

37. **Holiday party:** At the end of the year, we always threw a big ass Christmas party. The only way that you got to come is if you brought a referral or if you paid your bill on time. That day I made money. It cost me a little money to throw the party, but they came.

38. **Referral program:** See REFERRAL chapter.

39. **Gift Certificates**: I created gift certificates that I gave to realtors, mortgage brokers, businesses, and charities and they were all discount coupons off my activation fee. Some of them I sold to them, others I sold in kits. Some of them I gave to them, depending on where I was and if I needed more customers to come in. But

all of these people were out there bringing in new customers for me. So who are the referral partners in your business right now that you can give gift certificates to?

    a. Realtors

    b. Mortgage brokers

    c. Business

    d. Charity

40. **Monthly Contests - Activation Drawing:** You enter to win, one person is going to win, everybody else is going to get second place prize.

41. **Upgrade Requests:** During the process, we asked the customer for one additional up-sell.

42. **Takeaways In-Store:** Flyers inside stores.

43. **Takeaways in Cell Phone Boxes:** If you are shipping anything, there should be a takeaway in there – offers, coupons, and up-sells.

44. **Monthly Newsletter**

45. **Write Articles:** For websites and other publications.

46. **Joint Venture List:** You need to be putting together who sells before and after you to form partnerships – see "The Accelerators" chapter.

47. **Direct Mail to a Specific List:** I bought the following lists for FreshStart Telephone

    a. Poor credit

    b. Bankruptcy

    c. New movers

    d. Birthdays

    e. Insurance

48. **Display Ads:** Weekly newspaper.

49. **Give away samples:** Get up-sells with samples.

50. **Take Samples to a Fair/Expo/Seminar**

51. **Webinar:** To customers, to Joint Venture or OPC partners.

52. **Tele-Seminar**

53. **Other People's Thank You Page's Online:** After somebody buys from you online or buys from a similar joint venture partner, they can say "Thank you so much for buying." You can put your link on their thank you page. (ex. As a gift to you , there's a certificate for free activation of your telephone service)

54. **Other People's Thank You Gifts:** to their customers, my wedding group, photographer, caterer and DJ – give each a 'Thank You' gift for buying a discount coupon to each partner's business.

55. **Pod Casts on iTunes:** Put podcasts on the iTunes so people can download the information automatically. Read the articles to create your own.

56. **Social Media:** Facebook, LinkedIn, Twitter, YouTube – Be everywhere your prospects are.

57. **Craigslist Classified Ads**

58. **Banners on Competitor's Sites:** Forget SEO, if you are trying to get to the number one in your spot for a

certain search engine optimization, go to who is
number one and ask them can you buy a banner?

59. **Take one boxes inside partner's places:** This is very
simple. You can put a takeaway box in your partner's
place of business so that when they come in, they can
place their card inside or take a flyer.

60. **Place an Ad on the Delivery Pizza Boxes:** My private
clients who are insurance agents use this technique to
reach households in their area.

61. **Give Special Discounts for a Certain Group:**
Example - Military/Moms

62. **Happy Anniversary – to Clients:** From the first
order. Acknowledge that the customer has been there.

63. **Happy Anniversary – to the Business:** Create a
special for customers.

64. **Celebrity Night** – Invite local celebrity to your
location for autographs or get them as a guest speaker
online to a teleseminar or webinar. The use of

celebrity drives lots of traffic to offline and online businesses.

65. **Door prize event – the 1,000th customer wins**: Or the 7th customer to buy this today wins.

66. **Secret Red Envelope Offer:** After the customer buys, immediately give a red envelope. In the red envelope, there is a discount coupon off their next purchase to buy from you.

67. **Uniforms for Staff:** T-shirts to sell.

68. **Night at the Movies Promotion:** Get discounted tickets and have existing customers bring friends.

69. **New Movers:** Brand new people who move into the area, they have not picked their doctor, restaurants, dry cleaner, flower shop, etc.

70. **New Businesses**: New businesses that come into the area, you could sell them. People get new business licenses every day, you could get the list.

71. **Blood Donation Tie-In:** You could have a blood donation at your place of business and then get lots of traffic in and then you could sell them other things.

72. **Be a Charity Drop Off Point:** Be a charity drop-off point. We have Toys for Tots here or all kinds of other things you can set up your location to be a charity drop off.

73. **Have a Friends & Family Day for Your Staff:** If you have a staff, have a day for them to get a discount and their friends and family get a discount. I used to do this at FreshStart all the time. Not only did I have all of my employee's phone service, but I got all their friends and family too.

74. **Punch Cards:**

75. **Mystery Night – or Day – In Your Location:** You could have this if it is a mystery sale day so everybody that walks through the door gets a discount or gets something. Everybody who comes to your website that day gets a surprise bonus. They get to tell their

friends. You put a 'share' button so they can tell everybody on there.

76. **Parking Ticket Summons – Looks Like a Ticket but Really a Coupon:** If you go to where the shopping malls are and there are tons of cars, you put it underneath their windshield wiper so it looks like a ticket. They come over and go "Oh my gosh, I got a ticket" but it is really a summons and it goes, "Whew, here's the good news; it's not a parking ticket. It's really a discount coupon to come in and get a free cup of coffee." Fabulous to use over the holiday period because there are tons of people out. Check with your local authority for permission. .

77. **Team Sign Up Day (Soccer/Gymnastics) Be There with Coupons:** There is always a big day when they sign up for soccer or they sign up for football or they sign up for all these things for the kids. There are

going to be a ton of parents there. You can go there
and hand out coupons for your service.

78. **Report Card Incentives:** 'It's report card time so if
your children have 4 A's and a B at least or are on
honor roll, they can come in and get a free _____.' You
can always twist it any way you want so it will work in
your business.

79. **School Tour of your Location – Fieldtrips:** My kid
had several field trips and most of them have been at a
food place. Are you kidding me? We also went to the
planetarium last week and when we got there, they said
"Oh, don't miss the gift shop!" So my kid, "Mom can
I get a toy? Can I get a toy?" and all of the kids from
her school are there so that now each parent is trying to
outdo each other. They spent so much money in the
gift shop.

80. **After the Show Discounts:** After the movie, come in
with your ticket from the show and receive a discount.

81. **Ads During the Preview of the Movie – combine with after the show:** When you go to the movie theater there are place ads on the screen. Remember, no ads are expensive. They are only expensive when they do not work. You never go and buy a thirty year commitment or even a two year commitment. You buy a small ad. If it works, then you expand it, you get better. Remember, money is only used for pulling the trigger.

82. **Children's Birthday Club:** Not only can you have an adult birthday club but you can have a children's birthday club so that you can have parties. You can have all kinds of stuff, children's birthday club, love that.

83. **Theme Nights or Days in Your Business**: You can have Hawaiian nights and days. Get people to come in and have the special of the night. You could have Valentine's Night all that you want.

84. **One Year Group Coupon Book:** They have what we call the entertainment book here in Nevada. You can put an ad in there. Now they are online

85. **Group Buying Discounts Like Groupon & Living Social:** I love to use Groupon. Groupon is a great lead generator, but Groupon only works because you have to realize these people are ready for a deal. Groupon only works when you have your FOLLOW UP in place. If you do not have a FOLLOW UP in place, do not do Groupon because you are going to lose your shirt! But if you have got your FOLLOW UP in place to do the up-sell, to do the cross sale, to do the next sale, you have your newsletter already in place so that the newsletter is going out, you know what the next thing you are going to sell them is, then Groupon is fantastic because it costs you nothing. I get really excited about 85 Ways and when it starts to work and when the engine starts to move then you get one

customer from the online. You get three from the direct mail piece. You get two from the coupon. You get three from Facebook. You get one from the social media. You get three from the Tweet. You get one from the live seminar. It builds and builds and builds and your business changes dramatically when you work on all of the media.

The real sign of an entrepreneur is the ability to review each item on the list and determine how you can successfully use each one of these in your business.

Chapter 10: Let's Make This Simple - Only 3 Ways to Grow Your Business

The Three Ways to Grow Your Business – How to fight overwhelm

Chapter 9's lesson to implement simultaneously, can be overwhelming but the key to remember, there are only three ways to grow your business. First way to grow, get new customers and 90% of the business owners only do this one. The second way is get your existing customers to return more often.   The third way is get your existing customers to spend more when they are visiting you.

The Marketing Budget

To get new customers WAY #1, you should spend no more than 20% of your entire marketing budget even using those 85 ways. No more than 20%. I want you to spend the other 80% on doing newsletters, up-sells, discounts, gifts, special shopping days, reward days, nights to shop; all of the things that give a fabulous experience. Every new customer you get, you need to turn into two. It's not about getting somebody to buy one time. The way to have consistent months is to turn one customer into many.

The reason I do not begin the Million Dollar Equation with the 85 Ways is because business owners fall into the trap of forgetting about the second and third way to grow, expending all of their budget. I want you to nurture the new customer through the WOWing Welcome cycle because they will be your bread and butter. They are the ones that are going to catapult your business into greatness. This marketing ratio (20/new : 80/old) is the one thing that is going to change everything I promise you. Can you tell I am super passionate about that?

Building a million dollar business is about creating the strategy, laying out the foundation, so that they all work and then each piece of the puzzle develops.

Getting Customers to Come Back More Often

If you review Chapter 9, 85 Ways, there are several ways to get customers to come back more often such as punch cards and red envelopes, but can you see how sending birthday cards, having a children's birthday club or giving away free samples works too.

Getting Customers to Spend More on Each Visit

You see this in the classic McDonald's line – "Would you like fries with that?" At restaurants, they always offer you dessert, at the grocery store there are 43 items in the checkout lane. Online, Amazon.com pioneered the up-sell feature – customers who bought _____ also bought this, to encourage spending more on each visit. Other examples –

Spend $50 and get free shipping, buy 2 get one free, gift with

purchase of $100 or more. Combine your homeowners and

auto insurance for a discount. Ah ha!! Those sneaky business

people! But all of these ways increase the transaction size and

contribute to rapid growth.

PUTTING the PIECES together!

Your focus from the chapter is to:

1. *Take care of every customer with 80% of your marketing budget to turn one into two.*

2. *Create ways to bring the customer back and buy again.*

3. *Develop offers to increase every transaction size.*

4. *Maximize each interaction with the customer to generate word of mouth referrals, get them to return soon and spend more with each transaction.*

Chapter 11: The Accelerators

This chapter is all about the accelerators. These are like adding lighter fluid to the Million Dollar Equation. Once you perfect your GREAT SOLUTION, your TARGET MARKET, and your FOLLOW UP systems; now the key is to throw some lighter fluid onto it and have your business explode quickly. The accelerators are CI, AP or OPC. A lot of business owners prefer to start with the ACCELERATORS and then try to figure things out later, but I will caution you. It works best if you start by mastering your GREAT SOLUTION and your FOLLOW UP, because that is going to make the accelerators easier to implement, and easier to make money quickly.

Let me talk explain the accelerators, why the accelerators are so important and why you need to add a couple of accelerators to your business. Buying speed is the most important asset in your business right now in addition to your list of customers. However, I would much rather you take one and spend 90 days focusing on building it into your business. See what happens and then you can start building quickly on it. Then move on to the next accelerator.

ACCELERATOR #1 CI = Continuity Income

How to get customers to come back more often? Let's start with CI. CI is continuity income. Figure out a way, in your business, for the same customer can pay you either monthly, quarterly, or annually. Luckily FreshStart telephone has continuity income built in. The Secret: If I can keep billing every month, then my business would look dramatically different. As soon as I figured that piece out, it changed everything!

How can you offer continuity? What else is your TARGET MARKET looking for? I introduced continuity income to my private coaching client that sells basketball and tennis courts. Typically, his customer is not going to buy another basketball court. We created a new program which included cleaning of the basketball court, replacing the net, replacing some of the tile, making sure that the tile looks exactly like it did when it was first installed. We added continuity, a maintenance component to his business that has changed cashflow dramatically.

MDE Rule #22 – *Only way to get rich, sell continuity*

The only way to get rich, either you need to sell one big product for a whole lot of money or you need to add continuity to your business. Without continuity income in your business, sustaining growth is an uphill battle. Without continuity income the business will have good months, or will have bad months. Continuity solves that problem for you. Focusing on continuity income will build the business with fewer customers too!

Here are the questions you should ask to create continuity in your business:

1. *What are you normally giving away that you can create a continuity program with?*

2. *When is the customer asking for the next step?*

3. *When should your customer buy again? Can it be on automatic payments?*

4. *Does your product or service need maintenance?*

One of my private clients owns a studio and teaches dance classes. She gets tired of students coming with holes in their tights. So she created a 'Hole in my Tights' club. Now, when she sells the 'Hole in my Tights' club, she sells it as an up-sell or extension of when the customer registers for classes. Her sales pitch: "I hate to see holes in the dancer's tights and I don't want you running all over town." Invest today for $20 off. The Hole in my Tights club works really well and increases revenue each month by 17%.

ACCELERATOR #2 AP = Affluent Prices

How did you determine the prices for the products and services? I bet you are like most of my clients and you determined your prices based on one of the four ways.

1. You are the LOWEST – hoping that would bring in sales.

2. You surveyed your competition and you are somewhere between the highest and the lowest.

3. A flat percentage above the cost or amount you paid. You paid $17.00 and you charge $34.00.

4. The BAG theory – Best A** Guess. There is no exact formula to your pricing.

Each of these theories have major flaws and creates major havoc in the business.

The three most important determining factors in your pricing must be how much will my customer pay? What is my GREAT SOLUTION worth to the customer? Am I making enough profit to cover all expenses including overhead and internal marketing gifts?

The second portion of the accelerator is affluent prices. Do you know how much your customers will pay for your product? Have you tested different prices? Your top customers will pay more but, it is likely, you haven't asked them. Those 20% will equal the 80% that pay less.

MDE Rule # 24 – *Your customer should always be offered a GOOD, BETTER and BEST option.*

Your good option should be what you believe that it is worth to you right now. Your 'better' option, take your 'good' and add at least 30% to it. Your 'best' option should be the number if somebody actually takes it, you will jump up and down, do a toe touch a high five and have the best month ever. The majority of your customers will take the better option. Nobody ever wants to take the good, the bottom. Just by the fact that you are getting them to take the middle is going to give you a 30% raise from where you are right now and, if anybody takes the best, you are going to be phenomenally happy. You are going to be really excited and then you are going to go and change your prices again, trust me, because it gets good to you once it happens.

For example, I was in South Carolina last weekend at an event and I was with my coaching group. We pay a lot of money to get together and work on our businesses. There are always two of the members that refuse to wait in line or wait for anything. They pay for the best. You need to put in place in your business some way that your elite customers can choose that best option. People choose the best option for two reasons. First, because they like to feel special and the second is to buy speed, which also makes them feel special. There are people that are on your list that will pay for the best option. You need to know who they are and make sure that you have something in place for them to buy.

Getting your pricing right solves many challenges in your business. Having an affluent product or service will solve so many problems for you too. What can you add to your business that will warrant affluent pricing? One of the things, you can always add additional service or additional time with you. We talked about the 'Hole in my Tights' club - it happens after the sale, but it is a way to get affluent prices from the customer.

What else are your customers asking for? Even if you are not currently offering the product or service, seek out something else that the customers are asking for. When I initially review a private client's business, the first thing I add is continuity income to their business, which is number one. Even my optometrist, I went in and created a membership club for the optometrist so that they had the glasses of the month club. We invited them to secret sales. Even though they only need to come once every two years to get their eyes checked, we created a way that they would come at least once a quarter to check out the new styles.

The second thing I add Affluent Prices. Instead of having regular prices on the glasses, we stocked Jimmy Choo glasses, Gucci sunglasses, Maui Jims, all beautiful designer sunglasses that we would create a designer event. You may not be able to buy Jimmy Choo shoes for $800, but you can sure get their sunglasses for $259 and feel empowered.

ACCELERATOR #3 OPC = Other People's Customers

The final accelerator to quickly grow your business overnight is to find other people's customers (OPC). OPC is dramatically better than OPM, other people's money. Because with OPM, the only thing you can do is pay expenses. If somebody came in and offered you $10,000, the only thing you can do with that $10,000 is pay expenses. Even if you cash out your 401K, put a second mortgage on your house, got a loan, or use credit cards, all that is going to do is give you cash to pay bills or pay yourself. You can buy advertising, yet all it guarantees for you is exposure, but it can't guarantee that it is going to give you customers. Other people's customers will guarantee that, at least, you will get customers from it.

The second reason OPC works is buyers are buyers. I would be crazy to believe that you are only buying my marketing book. I bet you are buying other people's books and magazines, Entrepreneur, Inc., Fast Company. Good for you, I do too. Your behavior proves the point, that buyers are buyers. If they are buying a similar product or service somewhere else, they can and will still buy from you.

Easy OPC Tasks: Look to see who is selling to your customers before you or after you. Before they buy your product or service, what else are they buying? You want to take some time, close your eyes and get in a quiet place and think through this part of the business. One of my private clients is a caterer; she has a partnership with a wedding photographer, a wedding planner, and a wedding DJ. Between the four of them, here is what they do. When the photographer gets a call to shoot a wedding, the photographer as a thank you for using their service, gives a gift certificate which is a discount off of the caterer, the DJ and the planner's services. Each referred business gets a new customer; all four businesses are working together. Create your own network so that no matter what, when your partner gets a customer, you get one. Who in your business can you work together with to refer customers back and forth?

MDE Rule #25 – *For OPC Partners, see how you can help the OPC's Customers*

One of the ways that I was able to build FreshStart so quickly I approached the Payday Loan Center. I put my business inside the Payday Loan Center and when the customer entered, I was able to give the customers phone service. Here was the best thing; the Payday Loan Center wanted to make sure that their customers had a phone, so I solved the problem for them. Here is how we make sure they have a phone, we will put them on our phone service. Look to see how you can help the OPC Partner's customers.

Accelerator Review – To Build Quickly

1. Create some type of recurring product or service.

2. Create a good, better, or best product or service in your business.

3. Create your OPC relationships.

Chapter 12: What NEXT?

Let's RECAP and YOUR ACTION ITEMS

Alrighty then! Are you overwhelmed yet? You should be tingling all over. Dreaming of implementing your referral contest, redoing your communications to convey your Great solution, reactivating old customers and so much more.

Will you take the LEAP? Entrepreneurship is about risks. Every day you must take some type of risk in your business. Nothing is guaranteed or set in stone. Change is the only constant in business. How you deal with simple failures will determine if you ever get to deal with big successes. If work is not what you want to do, entrepreneurship is not for you. BUT, when you are alone in your office thinking about your business, here is the question I want you to consider. Are you ready to take action? Ready and Perfect NEVER come in business. In my coaching business I help entrepreneurs make money but most of the time it is helping them take action. Let me explain my CBI theory, which is Confidence leads to Belief and Belief leads to implementation. If I can give you enough confidence, I think that I can then give you the belief so that you will pull the trigger and continue to implement over and over and over. Some things work, some things do not, but that does not mean that you stop. It means that you keep going, because it will all work out in the end. Even cash flow issues all work themselves out as long as you put your head down and implement.

One of the things that I always get asked when I am speaking is how were you able to come back? How did you keep going? Quite frankly, every time I have a cashflow challenge, what I do is I close my eyes, I put my head down, and I start implementing. I do not ask any questions. I do not think is this right for me? What will people think? What will my mother think? I simply continue to implement.

After reading this book, you have the power to decide if this is just another business book – or are you truly ready to build a million dollar business. At this point, I have done my best. I have to say that I used to take it personal when people did not implement these strategies. BUT, now, I focus on giving you the best that I have and relinquish the control over to you.

Where there's change there's ACTION. Change for your business, for your life does not come from reading a book and living vicariously through me. The smallest steps mean progress. You may not see results quickly but keep moving and making steps. I will tell you that, there were so many struggles. Struggles after struggles. I learned an important lesson about success and failure. It feels almost the same. Entrepreneurship is a journey and one that if you are not celebrating each small success, it can be a long night, year, decade.

Yes, just like with the physician examples, I do take on some private clients, but that is very rare now. I do have online programs that are extensions of each of these chapters and concepts. They work the best once you implement. It is a support system to help you maneuver through the levels and evolution of your business. Each level of your business creates new drama and challenges.

I will be here with you all the way. Send me an update and let me know how you are doing at

http://www.MDENation.com

Last – may you experience even more success than me and I know that you can do it!

Much Success!

Richelle

Made in the USA
Lexington, KY
29 April 2018